DANGEROUS DRUGS

CAFFEINE AND ENERGY DRINKS

CHRISTINE PETERSEN

Cavendish Square
New York

Published in 2014 by Cavendish Square Publishing, LLC
303 Park Avenue South, Suite 1247, New York, NY 10010

LIBRARY OF CONGRESS CATALOGING-IN-PUBLICATION DATA
Petersen, Christine.
Caffeine and Energy Drinks / by Christine Petersen.
p. cm. — (Dangerous drugs)
Includes index.
ISBN 978-1-62712-378-5 (hardcover) ISBN 978-1-62712-379-2 (paperback)
ISBN 978-1-62712-380-8 (ebook)
1. Caffeine — Physiological effect — Juvenile literature. 2. Caffeine habit — Health aspects – Juvenile literature. 3. Energy drinks — United States — History — Juvenile literature. I. Petersen, Christine. II. Title.
RC567.5 P48 2014
615.785—dc23

EDITORIAL DIRECTOR: Dean Miller
SENIOR EDITOR: Peter Mavrikis
SERIES DESIGNER: Kristen Branch

Photo research by Kristen Branch

The photographs in this book are used by permission and through the courtesy of: Cover photo by © iStockphoto.com/© franckreporter; © iStockphoto.com/© franckreporter, 1; © Patti McConville/Alamy, 4; Tips Images/SuperStock, 7; © Christian Goupi/age fotostock, 8; © Rafael Campillo/age fotostock, 11; AP Photo/The Gleaner, Darrin Phegley, 14; akg-images/Newscom, 19; © JOSE OTO/BSIP/age fotostock, 21; Richard Levine/age fotostock/SuperStock, 23; © VOISIN/PHANIE/SARL PHANIE/age footstock, 25; Mikael Häggström/ Main side effects of Caffeine, 28; AP Photo/Lefteris Pitarakis, 30; Phil Dent/RedFerns/Getty Images, 33; © VOISIN/PHANIE/SARL PHANIE/age footstock, 35; Voisin/Phanie/SuperStock, 38; David Young-Wolff/The Image Bank/Getty Images, 40; leonello calvetti/Shutterstock.com, 42; BURGER/PHANIE/SARL PHANIE/age footstock, 47; © productsandbrands/Alamy, 49; CORBIS/CORBIS/age footstock, 51; GVictoria/Shutterstock.com, 42; Elena Elisseeva/Shutterstock.com, 54.

CONTENTS

CHAPTER ONE

Caffeine Everywhere

IT'S A HOT SUMMER DAY AND YOU'VE spent hours outside with friends. Time for a cool drink! A couple of centuries ago, thirsty kids had only a few beverage options. They might have drunk milk, fresh fruit juice, or tea. In cities, water was consumed only if it had been boiled to kill bacteria and other unhealthful pollutants. Step into a grocery or convenience store today and it becomes clear that the selections have changed drastically. You can choose from dozens of beverages.

Left: Many popular beverages sold in grocery and convenience stores contain caffeine, a chemical that has widespread effects on the human body.

Do you want flavoring or nutrients in your bottled water? Would you prefer chocolate milk to plain? What about juice in your iced tea? You can also select from a tempting display of soft drinks, sports drinks, smoothies, and energy drinks. The colorful line-up of bottles and cans may fill more than one aisle. Pop over to a coffee shop for more beverage options. There you'll find a selection of frosty blended drinks and frothy hot concoctions made with cocoa, coffee, or tea.

It's a Drug?!

Many of the drinks listed above are caffeinated. Caffeine is also found in a surprising number of foods. Do you ever have chocolaty cereals for breakfast or chocolate chip cookies after lunch? Those contain caffeine. Your scoop of coffee-flavored ice cream is caffeinated. So are candies, puddings, and cakes containing chocolate. Certain medicines also use caffeine as an ingredient.

We've all heard about caffeine, but what exactly is it? Caffeine occurs naturally in more than 60 plants that grow around the world. This chemical evolved in plants as a defense against insects and other small herbivores. When a hungry little animal takes a bite of the plant,

6

caffeine quickly enters its bloodstream. The chemical is carried into the central nervous system, which controls messages between the brain and body. Caffeine causes those messages to flow much more rapidly. The animal's nervous system is overwhelmed and it becomes paralyzed or dies. Some of these plants also produce theobromine and theophylline, chemicals that are related to caffeine and have similar effects.

Caffeine can also be made in laboratories. Because caffeine changes the body's natural way of functioning, it is considered a **drug**. Caffeine and other drugs that speed up the central nervous system are called **stimulants**. They include nicotine (found in cigarettes), cocaine, and amphetamine (also known as "speed").

Wild Caffeine

Coffee grows on small trees that thrive in warm climates near the equator. Small amounts of caffeine can be found in all parts of the coffee tree—from roots to

Coffee beans are hard seeds found inside the ripe fruits of coffee trees, which grow in tropical climates.

7

stems and leaves. But the highest concentration builds up in coffee seeds, or beans, which (like cherry pits) are found within the tree's bright red fruits. These beans are roasted, ground, and brewed in hot water. Each species of coffee tree produces beans with a unique flavor and concentration of caffeine.

Most teas are grown in Asia. All caffeinated teas are made from a single plant species called *Camellia sinensis*.

This worker is harvesting fresh leaves from *Camellia sinensis* plants on a tea farm in Madagascar.

Table 1. Caffeine content of some common US food products, 2009 (data from the Food and Drug Administration),

FOOD/BEVERAGE ITEM	SERVING SIZE (OZ)	SERVING SIZE (ML)	CAFFEINE CONTENT (MG)
Coffee, brewed	8	237	100-200
Coffee, decaffeinated	8	237	3-12
Espresso	1	30	30-90
Tea, black	8	237	40-120
Iced tea, bottled	16	473	10-42
Jolt Cola	12	355	72
Mountain Dew, regular or diet	12	355	54
Diet Coke	12	355	47
Pepsi	12	355	38
Coke Classic	12	355	35
Monster Energy	16	473	160
Red Bull	8.3	245	80
SoBe Essential Energy	8	237	48
Ben & Jerry's Coffee Heath Bar ice cream	8	237	84
Hershey's Special Dark chocolate bar	1.45	43	31
Hot cocoa	8	237	3-13

Black, oolong, and green are among the many tea varieties produced from this plant. Black teas are allowed to dry longer than other varieties, increasing their caffeine content. Herbal teas are made from the leaves of plants such as chamomile and mint that do not produce caffeine. The flavor of any tea results from the mix of different chemicals contained within its leaves. These are released when steeped in hot water.

Cocoa comes from the seed of the cacao tree. These small trees grow alongside shady rivers or beneath larger trees on farms in South America. After drying and roasting, the seeds are cracked open. The soft meat inside is used to make cocoa powder, cocoa butter, or chocolate. Cocoa has only a little caffeine. But it contains high levels of the related chemicals, theobromine and theophylline.

Several other stimulant plants, including the following, grow around the world and have been used to make hot or cold beverages.

- Yerba maté is a small tree related to holly. Native people of South America learned to make a drink from its leaves, which are soaked in hot water and sweetened with juice or spices.

Soft seed pods from cacao trees are the source of cocoa and a fatty oil useful in cooking and skin care products.

- Bright red guarana berries grow on vines in tropical South America.
- Spicy kola nuts are the fruit of kola trees, which grow in Africa. In some parts of Africa, people produce a beverage from kola nuts or chew them for their energizing effect.

The small black seeds of guarana are loaded with more caffeine than is found in coffee beans, along with theobromine and theophylline. Kola and maté also bring a double dose of stimulant, containing caffeine and theobromine. These stimulants have recently become popular as ingredients in **energy drinks**.

Energy drinks are much more highly caffeinated than soft drinks. There are dozens of brands, but you might recognize those that are most commons such as Monster, Red Bull, and Rock Star. Energy drinks usually contain high doses of **synthetic** caffeine (made in laboratories) combined with guarana, maté, or kola. Manufacturers often label these as "natural" sources of energy. Many people believe that natural equals healthy. But medical experts report that there are no health benefits to the

ingredients used in energy drinks. In fact, this is a potentially toxic brew. Very little research has been done to understand how these ingredients interact and affect the human body.

Research shows that about 90 percent of American adults and 75 percent of children regularly consume caffeine. On average, kids aged two to thirteen have more than 43 milligrams of caffeine daily. That's the equivalent of drinking a 12-ounce can of cola. Teens aged fourteen to twenty-one make a big jump in caffeine consumption. They average 107 mg per day—like having two servings of espresso, a powerful brew of coffee. Some people use much more caffeine than this.

A substance that is so widely used must be safe, right? Not necessarily. Regular use of caffeine may affect your sleep and reduce your ability to concentrate at school. It can make you jittery and grumpy, impacting relationships with family and friends. Caffeine is addictive, so it's hard to stop using once you start. And this drug has been shown to harm brain and heart development in young people. These are just a few of the reasons to think twice before you use caffeine.

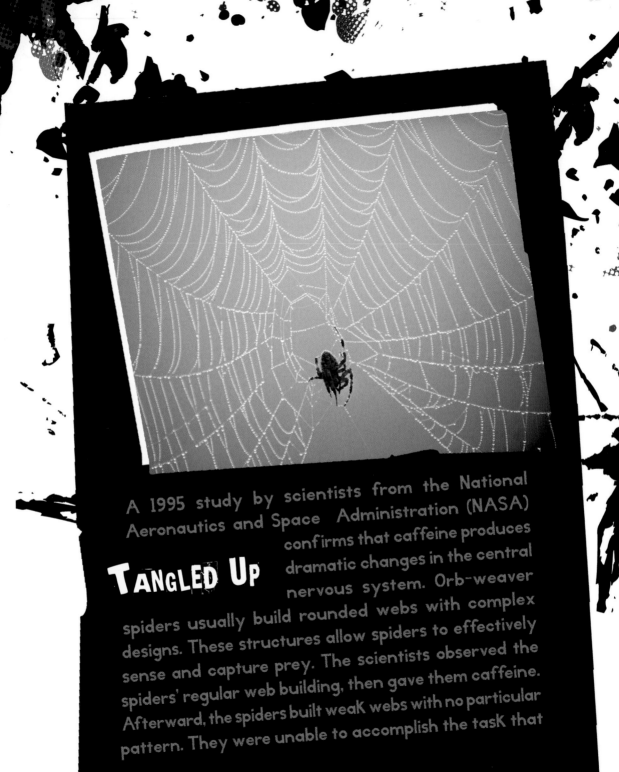

A 1995 study by scientists from the National Aeronautics and Space Administration (NASA) confirms that caffeine produces dramatic changes in the central nervous system. Orb-weaver

TANGLED UP

spiders usually build rounded webs with complex designs. These structures allow spiders to effectively sense and capture prey. The scientists observed the spiders' regular web building, then gave them caffeine. Afterward, the spiders built weak webs with no particular pattern. They were unable to accomplish the task that usually takes up most of their time and energy. Without a good web, a spider cannot catch food and will die. You're not a spider, but caffeine also affects you in significant and unpredictable ways.

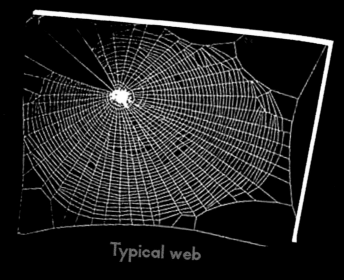

Typical web

Spider on Caffenine

CHAPTER TWO

More, More, More

HAVE YOU EVER MADE A CUP OF HOT cocoa then left the unwashed cup sitting on the counter for a day or two? The liquid dries, forming a crusty residue inside the cup. In the ruins of a once-great city called San Lorenzo, scientists have found ancient cups, bowls, and jars containing that same kind of dried-up cocoa. San Lorenzo was home to the Olmec people, Mexico's first great civilization. Those containers are about 3,800 years old.

The Olmec were possibly the first people to cultivate cacao trees and to make a hot drink from the plant's seeds. In later centuries, Aztec people of Mexico gave chocolate its name—*xocoatl* (shah-coh-ah-tul). The Aztecs believed this substance had magical powers, including the ability to make

people happy. Priests sometimes gave out the precious hot drink before important religious ceremonies. *Xocoatl* helped to calm those who had been chosen for sacrifice to the gods.

Tea drinking dates back at least 2,500 years. Chinese philosopher Lao Tzu said that tea was like jade, one of the most valued minerals in Chinese culture. He believed tea might be one of the ingredients in a mixture that could bring eternal life. Confucius is said to have written that tea "awakens thought and prevents drowsiness." That's an accurate description of caffeine's stimulant effects at low **doses**. Early on, tea was made in powder rather than leaf form. Only royalty and wealthy people were allowed to drink it.

There are no written records or historical objects to prove the distant history of coffee. Some stories say it came from Ethiopia, a country in northeastern Africa. By the fifteenth century, coffee trees were farmed on the Arabian Peninsula. Through trade, popularity of the bean spread to countries and kingdoms around the Mediterranean Sea.

In the sixteenth and seventeenth centuries, European merchants and explorers traveled around the world to trade and conquer new lands. They brought back many goods and foods. Among them were cacao, tea, and coffee. These flavors quickly became popular in European cities. By the mid-1600s, more than 300 coffeehouses had opened in the city of London alone. Men gathered in these establishments to enjoy a hot drink and exchange news of the day. Women held tea parties to visit with friends in their homes. Similar establishments began to appear as cities were built in the young American colonies. Especially in Boston, coffeehouses became meeting places for patriots who were unhappy to be governed by a distant British king and parliament.

Those conversations turned angry in 1768, when Britain imposed a tax on many goods imported to the colonies—including tea. On December 16, 1773, a group of colonists snuck aboard three ships in Boston Harbor and dumped 92,000 pounds (41,730 kg) of tea overboard so it could not be sold. The Boston Tea Party was among the first rebellious acts that led to the American Revolution. Because colonists had so little access to tea during this period, many became coffee drinkers. That trend has never changed.

You might wonder about the history of soft drinks. In 1767, British chemist Joseph Priestly made the first carbonated water. About 50 years later, American inventor John Mathews built a machine that produced

On December 16, 1773, colonists dressed as Mohawk Indians snuck aboard ships and tossed their cargo of tea into Boston Harbor in protest of high British taxes.

carbonated water in a soda fountain. Soda water was considered healthful. Pharmacies set up fountains and sold carbonated drinks flavored with herbs and juices. Georgia pharmacist Dr. John Stith Pemberton developed a new soda flavor in 1886. He called it Coca-Cola. Later versions of this recipe included caffeine as an ingredient. Manufacturers soon developed a way to make glass bottles in factories (rather than blowing them singly and by hand). Soft drinks were made by the thousands and sold in many grocery stores. Americans could have a soda any time.

AN ACQUIRED TASTE

Soft drink manufacturers regularly add caffeine to their products. The practice is so common that the U.S. Food and Drug Administration (FDA) has limited use of caffeine in soft drinks at levels up to 71 milligrams per 12 ounces. Caffeine is supposedly used to improve flavor. But researchers at Harvard University wondered whether these companies might have another, more subtle reason for including caffeine in beverages.

In 2011, Dr. Jennifer Temple and her team at Harvard tested a group of adolescents, ages twelve to seventeen. The teens were asked to taste soft drinks each day for four days. Each drink contained a different amount of caffeine, or sometimes none at all. Participants never knew what they were getting because each sample was unmarked. Teens indicated how well they liked each beverage after sampling. The results were clear. Kids didn't show much of a change in their opinion of beverages containing no caffeine or just a little of the chemical. Those who drank highly caffeinated drinks ranked them highly. In fact they liked those beverages even more after four days.

Caffeine has somewhat of a bitter taste. As people drink more of it, they get used to this flavor. They apparently learn to like it. Added caffeine may not only improve the flavor of a beverage, but even lead people to choose it over drinks containing no caffeine. This information could influence the way drink manufacturers develop and market their products.

The Caffeine Routine

Adults often start the day by making a cup of coffee. Why do they like it so much? Most would say that they enjoy the taste—and that it helps them wake up in the morning. This caffeine routine is not limited to grown-ups. Marilyn M. Beard, MD, who specializes in pediatrics, wondered whether kids also have a preference for caffeine. During routine check-ups, Dr. Beard conducted a survey of 108 patients ages nine to seventeen. She asked them to list their four favorite drinks. (What would your

Studies show that young people learn to enjoy the flavor of caffeinated drinks.

answers be?) Her patients ranked soft drinks, coffee or tea, and energy drinks far above milk and juice. Most kids also listed water, but some drank brands of vitamin water that are caffeinated.

There are many reasons why young people use caffeine including:

- they like the flavor,
- caffeine provides a sensation they like, or it keeps them alert, and
- friends or peers are using it.

Many of Dr. Beard's patients could describe the effects of caffeine. It "gets my day going," explained one teen. "I keep wanting more of it," said another. Dr. Beard was concerned when she realized her patients "were not sure which beverages other than coffee [such as colas and tea drinks] contained caffeine and which did not." That lack of knowledge puts young people at risk. They can easily become ill after unknowingly consuming too much caffeine.

Truth in Advertising?

Dr. Beard is one of many experts having raised another concern about caffeine and kids. "It appears that

caffeine has been glamorized," she comments. Think about the advertisements you've seen for soft drinks and energy drinks. They show celebrities holding up the product, or young people involved in thrill-seeking activities and then stopping to get a "boost" with a caffeinated beverage. These ads give the impression that caffeine allows you to accomplish anything. Makers of these products also sponsor high-energy sports competitions such as snowboarding and surfing, skateboaring, and motocross. This is a sales technique called "bandwagon." It relies on people's desire to join the crowd and be popular. Bandwagon ads really work. Thirty to 50 per-

Advertisements can make us feel like we don't fit in unless we buy certain products.

cent of American children, adolescents, and young adults consume energy drinks.

But there's another side to the story. In the United States, laws only require drink manufacturers to list synthetic caffeine that has been added for flavor. Plant-based stimulants such as coffee, tea, and guarana do not require labeling. For that reason, you can't easily tell how much stimulant you're getting. Experts calculate that energy drinks contain up to 16 mg of stimulant per ounce. At that concentration, a typical 20-ounce bottle delivers 335 mg of stimulant—more than the recommended daily dose for adults. Young people have a much stronger reaction to caffeine because they weigh less. To be safe, children and teens should consume less than 100 mg of caffeine per day.

More and more people are being admitted to emergency rooms for illness caused by energy drinks. The number of cases has doubled to almost 21,000 per year since 2007. Poison control centers also receive calls about energy drink abuse. In the first five months of 2013, almost two-thirds of those calls were about children or teens under the age of eighteen. **Adverse reactions** to energy drinks range from mild vomiting or headache to extreme mental confusion, seizures, and death. Coffee drinks can also be highly caffeinated. You may even become ill after drinking a lot of sodas or tea in a short period of time.

24

Energy drinks rarely label the amounts of caffeine and other stimulants in the product.

Food and drink manufacturers aren't going to remind you that caffeine is a drug. Their job is to sell a product. It's up to you to learn the risks. Information allows you to make choices that will protect your health.

CHAPTER THREE

Caution

YOU MAY HAVE HEARD THE TERM "caffeine buzz" or even felt this sensation when the drug is in your body. But how does caffeine cause its effects?

Breaking it Down

Imagine you're drinking a cola. Each gulp slides down the long tube of your esophagus, which empties into your stomach. The stomach's job is to soften and begin digesting food. Cola is already a liquid, so it moves quickly into the intestines. Here, food is broken down further into water and nutrients. These molecules can pass through the walls of the intestine into tiny capillaries that join up with larger vessels. Like nutrients, caffeine molecules are able to pass into the bloodstream through the intestines.

Within about 45 minutes, 99 percent of the caffeine that was in the cola has entered your bloodstream.

Your liver has the important job of filtering blood. It breaks down nutrients, turning some into sugar that can be stored or used for energy. The liver also removes toxins. Caffeine falls into that category. It takes the liver about four hours to remove half of the caffeine you consumed. What about the remaining caffeine? Four hours are needed to clear out half of that. This process continues until all of the caffeine is gone. You get the point: Caffeine stays in your body for quite a while.

The Buzz

In the hours before it is all broken down, caffeine has widespread effects on your body. Its work begins in the central nervous system (CNS). The CNS, including the brain and spinal cord, is your body's control station. It tells your organs how to function and lets you respond to information collected by your senses.

The CNS must also ensure that you sleep. It does this by producing a chemical called adenosine. Adenosine attaches to nerves on docking sites called receptors. No other chemical produced by the body will fit on those

Main side effects of
Caffeine

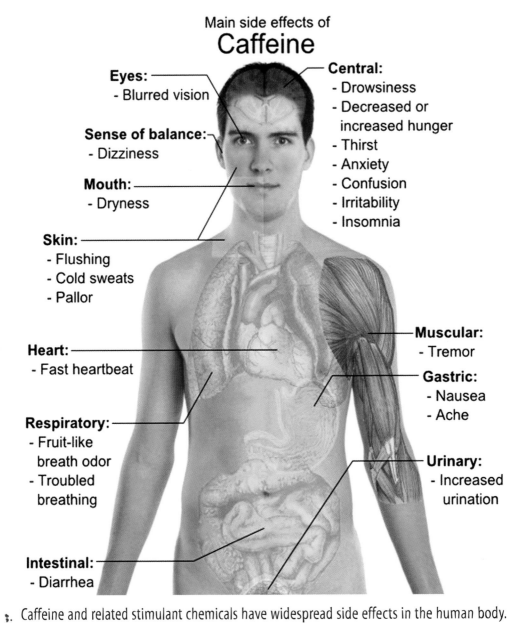

Eyes:
- Blurred vision

Sense of balance:
- Dizziness

Mouth:
- Dryness

Skin:
- Flushing
- Cold sweats
- Pallor

Heart:
- Fast heartbeat

Respiratory:
- Fruit-like breath odor
- Troubled breathing

Intestinal:
- Diarrhea

Central:
- Drowsiness
- Decreased or increased hunger
- Thirst
- Anxiety
- Confusion
- Irritability
- Insomnia

Muscular:
- Tremor

Gastric:
- Nausea
- Ache

Urinary:
- Increased urination

Caffeine and related stimulant chemicals have widespread side effects in the human body.

receptors. Adenosine is their perfect match, like a key in a lock. When an adenosine molecule clicks into place, it slows down the activity of that nerve. Little by little, adenosine builds up throughout the day. In response, your energy and thoughts gradually slow down and you become sleepy.

Coincidentally, caffeine molecules have a shape that is similar to adenosine. When you consume caffeine, molecules of the drug "park" in adenosine receptor sites. This blocks adenosine so you don't get sleepy. At the same time, caffeine increases the activity of nerves. That is why caffeine and related chemicals (such as theobromine and theophylline found in chocolate, maté, and other sources) are called stimulants. They cause messages to move faster than normal between cells of the central nervous system. That's not all. Caffeine and related stimulants make your body release chemicals that are normally present only when you feel stress or fear. Together, these chemical changes produce the caffeine "buzz": faster breathing and heart rate, a greater sense of alertness, and more energy.

Too Much

Watch out! There is a fine line between the amount of caffeine that makes you alert and the dose that can leave

Poor Sports?

To qualify for the Olympics, athletes must be among the very best at their chosen sports. They are expected to achieve peak performance through dedication and practice, not by using drugs. An organization called the World Anti-Doping Agency (WADA) works to prevent the use of performance-enhancing drugs in Olympic-level sports. WADA regularly tests athletes' blood and urine for steroids, marijuana, and other drugs. These tests also look for stimulants such as caffeine.

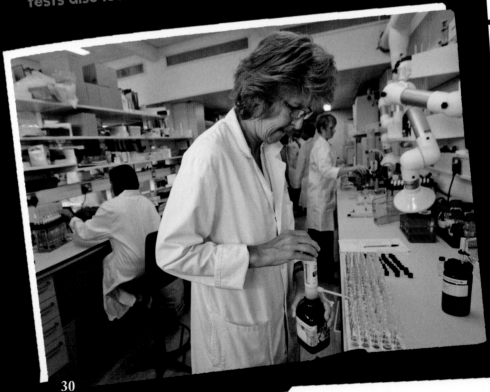

About 21,000 tests were conducted after national and international competitions held between 2004 and 2008. Almost three-quarters of the samples contained caffeine. Of those, 124 showed excessive amounts of caffeine. The number may seem small and unimportant. But those players were using enough stimulants to provide an unfair advantage in their endurance or performance. What if those people went on to the Olympics and won gold medals? Is it fair to other athletes if winners get energy from stimulant drugs?

WADA is concerned that caffeine use has increased among the world's best athletes over the past few years. The problem is greatest in highly competitive sporting events such as bicycling, rowing, and triathlons because players must keep their energy up for long periods to win. WADA will continue to watch the situation. Players may face a ban on caffeine if use increases. The National Collegiate Athletic Association (NCAA) has already taken that step. The more than 1,000 colleges and universities that participate in NCAA sporting events are prohibited from giving energy drinks to student athletes.

you feeling ill. Too much caffeine causes **intoxication**. It's the buzz "gone bad." While intoxicated, you may feel so twitchy and distracted that it's hard to sit still or concentrate. Excess caffeine can make your heart feel as if it's racing or skipping in your chest. When intoxicated, you're unlikely to get any sleep for several hours. And you won't be able to go too far from a bathroom, because caffeine causes you to urinate more often and may upset your stomach or intestines. Stimulants such as caffeine also affect your mood. While a little can make you feel cheerful, excess caffeine often leads to crankiness. Common symptoms of caffeine intoxication include:

- nervousness
- poor concentration
- upset stomach
- increased urination
- flushed face
- irregular or rapid heartbeat
- difficulty falling asleep
- headache

Musician Dave Grohl knows the risks of caffeine intoxication. In 2010, he was hospitalized after experiencing chest pains. The drummer, who performs with three

well-known bands, had a new-born baby at the time. His busy schedule made it hard to get more than two or three hours of sleep each night. Grohl had been using coffee to stay alert. His chest pain was a sign of **overdose**—Grohl had taken more of the drug than his body could handle. Fortunately, his symptoms were caught in time. Changing his caffeine consumption allowed him to recover.

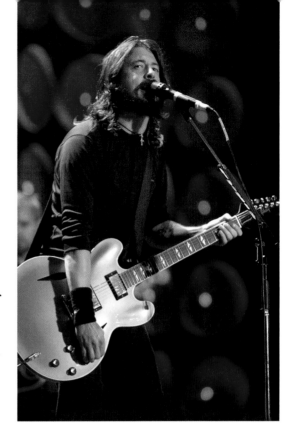

Musician Dave Grohl experienced the dramatic symptoms of caffeine overdose in 2010.

Risky

Energy drinks have become increasingly popular among young people, and they often contain high doses of caffeine. But did you know that some energy drinks include alcohol? Caffeinated alcoholic beverages (CABs) may have higher levels of alcohol than beer. Alcohol **depresses**, or slows down, the central nervous system—the opposite of stimulants. Symptoms include dizziness, confusion, and slurred speech. Some people think that caffeine reduces these effects. In fact, caffeine only hides the symptoms of alcohol intoxication. That's a risky situation. Users believe they are alert, but their brains and bodies continue to react in slow and clumsy ways. Here's another serious problem. People who drink CABs are three times more likely to **binge**. They consume one after another in a short period of time, adding to the risk of adverse reactions or risky behaviors. The Centers for Disease Control and Prevention report that more than 79,000 deaths each year are connected to excessive alcohol consumption. More than half of those deaths result from binge drinking.

Even without alcohol, caffeine seems to make young people more impulsive. That means they take risks without thinking through the possible consequences beforehand. The higher the dose, the more impulsive young caffeine users become. They may drive recklessly or get into fights. Studies also show that teens using a lot of caffeine are more likely to begin smoking and may try illegal drugs. Younger children also show impulsive behavior after having chocolate, soft drinks, and other caffeinated products. They may feel hyper or out of control. Caffeine has not been diagnosed as a cause of attention-deficit hyperactivity disorder (ADHD). But some researchers worry that the disorder

has symptoms that overlap with caffeine intoxication. As a result, some children may be mistakenly diagnosed with ADHD. These children might feel and behave better if caffeine was taken out of their diets.

It's not that using caffeine turns you into a bad kid. But adolescence is already a challenging time of life. You are still figuring out how to choose between right and wrong. Portions of the brain that control reasoning and impulses don't fully develop until about the age of twenty-five. When you add

Consuming too much caffeine may cause adolescents to become impulsive, angry, or hyperactive.

caffeine, alcohol, or other drugs to the mix, it can be almost impossible to stay in control of your behavior.

Stop Signs

Some people simply can't use caffeine at all. Pay attention to your body to learn if you are part of this group. If you feel intoxicated after just a small amount of caffeine, stay away from it. Your body may be especially sensitive to this drug and will never react well to its effects. If you have an anxiety disorder or fibromyalgia, caffeine can worsen your symptoms. Caffeine can also decrease the effectiveness of certain antibiotics. Always check with your doctor before using caffeine if you take prescription medications or have a health condition.

In December 2012, a 14-year-old girl from Maryland drank large cans of a popular energy drink two days in a row. On the second day, her heart suddenly changed its rhythm. The young teen collapsed, and died six days later. Her family had been aware that she had a heart condition, but no one in the family was aware that caffeine could set off a life-threatening attack. Over the past few years, the FDA has received other reports of deaths linked to energy drinks. A 19-year-old California man suffered a heart attack in 2012. He had been a regular energy drink user, consuming two cans per day for three years before his death. Some victims have been lucky enough to survive adverse reactions including heart attack, tremors, and severe abdominal pain. Perhaps we need to change our thinking and begin to treat caffeine with more caution.

CHAPTER FOUR

That Hurts

ADULTS OFTEN USE CAFFEINE IN THE morning. Teens are more likely to use it during the daytime or evening. Energy drink companies tell you their products will help you recover after playing sports. It's tempting to use caffeine to stay alert for long study sessions. The drug also promises longer nights of gaming, social networking, and television.

You've already read that caffeine has many effects on your body. It halts your natural build-up of chemicals that lead to sleep, and produces other chemicals that cause symptoms similar to fear. Caffeine intoxication can upset your stomach, alter your behavior, and even cause heart problems. Another danger of caffeine use is sleep loss.

37

It's risky to drink caffeinated beverages at night because they may deprive you of sleep.

38

In adolescence, the body's sleep cycle changes. Many teens find it hard to fall asleep before 11 p.m. Your brain needs sleep to store all the new things you learned each day. Your body needs it to fight off illness and repair injuries. Missing one night's sleep will leave you yawning the next day. Regular sleep loss can make you grumpy, distracted, and clumsy. Using caffeine adds to these challenges—especially when you use it to stay up late. Your brain may grab sleep in the middle of class or while you should be studying for a test. Driving while sleep-deprived is the equivalent of getting behind the wheel drunk. Your brain and body just can't react quickly enough to prevent accidents. It's just as dangerous to ride with someone else who isn't well rested.

Despite these problems, only about 15 percent of American teens get 8.5 hours of sleep each night. That's the minimum amount recommended. Adolescents grow and change so quickly that they really need at least 9.25 hours of sleep to stay healthy.

Bad to Worse

Even if it doesn't steal your sleep, caffeine use can impact your health in other ways. An ulcer is like an open sore in the stomach or upper intestine. Most ulcers are caused by

Sports drinks are not caffeinated, but you might think twice before choosing them. The American Academy of Pediatrics has these reminders:

· Electrolytes, including sodium and potassium, are advertised as important ingredients of sports drinks. It's true that you sweat out these salts when exercising. Sports

A Closer Look at Sports Drinks

drink companies claim that you need to consume electrolytes to regain energy. In fact, few people exercise hard enough to require electrolyte replacement. Plain water and healthy food do the trick.

- Lots of people choose sports drinks even when they have not been exercising. These drinks contain high levels of carbohydrates that can contribute to obesity.
- Citric acid used to flavor sports drinks can break down the minerals in enamel on the surface of teeth, causing tooth decay.

Pediatricians have a simple solution when you need to remain hydrated: drink water before, during, and after exercising and playing sports.

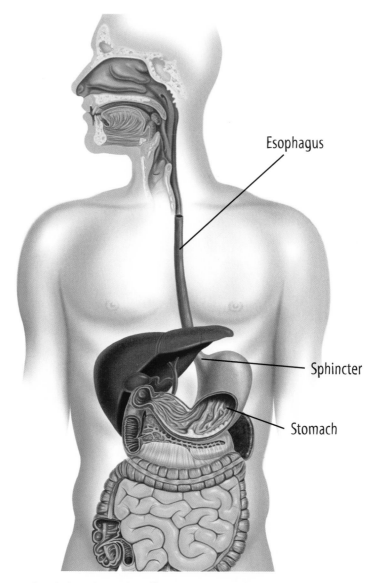

Esophagus

Sphincter

Stomach

Drinking too much caffeine can cause ulcers, heartburn, and other uncomfortable health conditions affecting the digestive system.

a bacterial infection. Caffeine increases the production of stomach acids, which increases the pain and makes it hard for the ulcer to heal. Whatever your favorite caffeinated beverage—sodas, tea, coffee, cocoa, or energy drinks— regular use also puts you at risk of heartburn. Caffeine and related stimulants relax smooth muscles throughout your body. That includes the muscle between your esophagus and stomach. This muscle, the lower esophageal sphincter, usually acts like a gate. It opens only to allow a mouthful of food to enter the stomach, and then closes. If you drink too much caffeine, the muscle relaxes slightly, leaving a tiny opening. Acidic, partially digested food from your stomach can then slip by and flow backward up the esophagus. That creates a burning sensation known as heartburn. It's not just a feeling. Strong stomach acids can actually damage your esophagus if heartburn continues untreated.

People sometimes use caffeine when trying to lose weight. Caffeine can slightly reduce the feeling of hunger. It may cause fat to burn a little faster, and it certainly makes users urinate more frequently. All of these factors contribute to weight loss, but it would probably take a lot of caffeine to produce noticeable results. That could cause other serious health problems. Caffeine users should think seriously about the opposite problem, of gaining weight. Energy drinks, sodas, and coffee drinks might taste good. But these and other caffeinated beverages often contain "empty" calories that take the place of nutritious foods like dairy, vegetables, and healthy grains in the diet. Adolescents are still growing and need a balanced diet, not fillers.

Hard to Let Go

Think back over the past week. Can you list all the caffeinated foods and drinks you've had? Ask an adult and a friend the same question then compare your answers. How did you feel after consuming those products? If you're not a regular user, caffeinated foods and beverages can cause noticeable side effects every time. People who consume caffeine daily may not feel any reaction. This is called **tolerance**. It means that your body has adjusted to the changes caused by caffeine. A larger dose of the drug is required, then more and more, to create the same response or experience.

Long-term use of caffeine can also lead to **dependence**. Dependence is an emotional or physical need for a drug. Medical experts use several criteria to diagnose caffeine dependence:

• reaching a point of tolerance,

44

- experiencing **withdrawal** symptoms when reducing or stopping use of the drug,
- unsuccessful attempts to reduce or quit using the drug, and
- using the drug despite knowing that it can cause physical or mental health problems.

Researchers at the University of Minnesota found that adolescents who consume caffeine daily are vulnerable to dependence, just like adults. Of 36 teens in the study, more than 40 percent said they had reached tolerance—after using caffeine for a while, they had to increase the dose to feel its effects. About the same number reported that they had tried and failed to quit using caffeine. One-sixth of the group admitted they used caffeine despite knowing it is unhealthy. Eight-tenths of the teens in the study had experienced withdrawal.

During withdrawal from caffeine, people often feel exhausted, anxious, and headachy. Withdrawal passes as the body adjusts to functioning without the drug, but it can be a miserable few days. Some people don't make it through. They resume the use of caffeinated drinks just to relieve the symptoms. If possible, it's better never to begin using caffeine or at least to keep daily use at a minimum.

CHAPTER FIVE

Decaffeinated

CAFFEINE IS EVERYWHERE IN OUR
society, yet millions of people choose to live without it.
Others enjoy small amounts now and then but avoid daily
or large doses. How can you find that kind of balance? It's
a matter of choice.

Resisting

Sodas may be easily accessible to you every day, in the fridge
at home or in vending machines at school. You are probably
offered soft drinks at parties, and caffeinated drinks are
sold at restaurants everywhere. Friends might gather at a
coffee shop or grab energy drinks at an after-school hang-

46

Peer pressure influences many of our decisions, down to simple things like the beverages we drink.

out. Reducing caffeine in your diet requires breaking old habits. But it's also an opportunity to try new things.

Peer pressure is a more subtle force. The message is intense: "You must look and behave like others in order to have friends. If not, you will miss out on life's best experiences and opportunities." Most of the time, peers have only as much power as we give them. But that can be hard to see in the moment. This is especially true because our brains learn primarily by imitation. When we see others act a certain way, it can be hard to resist doing the same thing. Even adults struggle to overcome peer pressure.

Soured on Sweeteners

You may be tempted to choose diet colas or other beverages that contain artificial sweeteners. Think twice before you drink. Removing sugar does not affect the level of caffeine in a product. In some cases, diet drinks contain higher levels of caffeine than their sugared counterparts. For example, 47 mg of caffeine are added to the 12-ounce can of Diet Coke while the same amount of Coke Classic contains 35 mg of caffeine.

Artificial sweeteners such as aspartame, saccharin, and sucralose are intended to provide a sweet flavor without the fattening effect of sugar. Yet studies suggest that sweeteners may cause people to gain weight over time. Regular use of artificial sweeteners has also been associated with type-2 **diabetes** and heart disease. In type-2 diabetes, blood sugar levels are too high. The body usually makes insulin to break down glucose. But people with type-2 diabetes do not produce insulin normally. They can develop many symptoms and related health problems. Metabolic syndrome has also been linked to artificial sweeteners. This is a collection of health problems including high blood pressure, high cholesterol, and elevated blood sugar. Belly fat is another sign of metabolic syndrome. Adults with these risk factors are at much greater risk of heart disease, stroke, and diabetes.

These health issues might seem unimportant to people your age. But give it some thought. The health habits you establish now will affect your behaviors into the future.

Nutrition Facts
Valeur nutritive

Per 1 can (355 mL)
pour 1 canette (355 mL)

Amount Teneur		% Daily Value % valeur quotidienne
Calories / Calories 0		
Fat / Lipides 0 g		
Sodium / Sodium 50 mg		0 %
Carbohydrate / Glucides 0 g		2 %
Sugars / Sucres 0 g		0 %
Protein / Protéines 0.1 g		

Not a significant source of saturated fat, trans fat, cholesterol, fibre, vitamin A, vitamin C, calcium or iron.

Source négligeable de lipides saturés, lipides trans, cholestérol, fibres, vitamine A, vitamine C, calcium et fer.

APPLICABLE/RETOURNER POUR REMBOURSEMENT LÀ OÙ APPLICABLE

URIC AND CITRIC ACID, ASPARTAME (CONTAINS PHENYLALANINE), FLAVOURS, SODIUM BENZOATE, E, COLORANT AU CARAMEL, ACIDE PHOSPHORIQUE ET CITRIQUE, ASPARTAME (CONTIENT DE LA

49

Remember this: Health and fitness are respected in our culture. Peers may question your choice to give up caffeine. Simply reply that you prefer healthier drinks. Back that up with your actions. Choose plain water, juices, milk, or fresh-fruit smoothies with no added supplements. Herbal teas are also delicious, iced or hot. The more often you make this choice, the easier it will become. Other friends may decide to join you. If not, it's okay to be different. Eventually, you may meet new friends who have also chosen health over habit. Like you, they will understand that you don't need caffeine to lead an energetic and fulfilling life.

It helps to have support when you make such a big change in your behavior. Just like teens, adults are often unaware of the risks from caffeine use. Consider sharing your knowledge with family members. The dinner table is a great place to start those conversations. You can suggest replacing soft drinks with healthier beverages at mealtime. You might even ask for a reusable water bottle. It will fit in your backpack and can be easily refilled throughout the day. Your family will save a lot of money when they stop buying disposable bottles or cans of soda and energy drinks. Drinking from a reusable bottle also helps the environment. Less than 30 percent of plastic bottles are

You can make fresh-squeezed juice at home as a healthy, delicious alternative to caffeinated beverages.

recycled every year. Your healthy choice is a great example for younger siblings. They look up to you and will imitate your actions, bad or good.

Make That Change

Don't quit suddenly if caffeine is a regular part of your diet. Remember that caffeine withdrawal symptoms can

A food diary can help you identify the sources of caffeine in your diet and make manageable choices for change.

be pretty uncomfortable. Spend a few days tracking how much caffeine you consume. This can require some research but it's worth the time. You'll probably be surprised at the results. Federal law requires that manufacturers list caffeine when it is added to their products, but they do

not have to disclose the amount. Until 2013, all energy drinks were considered dietary supplements. While in this category, companies did not have to show whether the product contained caffeine or how much. Several energy drinks have chosen to be relisted as beverages. Now you will see them in the soft drink aisle alongside sodas and flavored waters. Caffeine will appear in the list of ingredients, but this does not tell you anything about other stimulants such as guarana, maté, or kola. Many coffee shops provide nutrition information on request. You can contact manufacturers or use the Internet to find the caffeine content of most other products.

Whatever amount of caffeine you usually consume, cut it in half every few days. Replace the caffeine with water and other nutritious beverages. At the same time, look at your diet. Grains, vegetables, and fruits provide protein, vitamins, and minerals that are like fuel for your body. By eating healthy foods every day and staying hydrated with water before and after exercise, your body should maintain its natural balance. You will have plenty of energy to participate in all the sports and activities you enjoy.

Here are a few additional tips for maintaining an energetic, caffeine-free lifestyle:

Exercise, water, and a healthy diet are a great recipe for maintaining your energy level without the side effects of stimulants.

54

- Get plenty of exercise and outdoor time. Movement and fresh air are natural sources of energy.
- Spend time with friends and family. Positive relationships provide emotional energy.
- Remember that adolescents need about 9.25 hours of sleep a night. A regular sleep schedule will help you feel focused and alert.

Pay attention to your body and emotions. You should feel terrific after cutting caffeine from your diet and getting into these healthier, energy-boosting routines. If not, you might want to see a doctor to identify other reasons for your low energy. Depression can make you tired. Certain health conditions also sap your strength. The effects of caffeine might have hidden or worsened those symptoms. With treatment, you will probably be able to regain your oomph and enthusiasm.

Showing Restraint

Individuals must make their own choices about caffeine use. But as a society we must face a larger question. Why is a potentially harmful drug available to young people? Parents, doctors, and others are finally beginning to demand an answer. Remember the two teens you read about earlier that died in 2012 after consuming energy drinks? The parents of those teens are suing the beverage company. San Francisco's city attorney, Dennis Herrera, also filed a lawsuit against Monster Beverage Corp, which manufactures the Monster energy drink. Herrera and the families charge that Monster did not provide warnings about the risks of its products. Herrera points out that the company encourages youths to "chug down" its products and uses children as young as six in some of its advertisements. Makers of soft drinks, national coffee chains, and other businesses must also begin to think about the effects of their products on children.

The FDA has begun to take notice of problems with caffeine. In 2010, the agency banned caffeinated alcoholic beverages because of the proven risks from mixing caffeine and alcohol. It has also noticed a recent trend in which manufacturers add caffeine to unexpected foods. Now just about anything may be caffeinated, from waffles and oatmeal to potato chips and marshmallows. The Wrigley's company recently released a line of caffeinated

gum. Each piece had as much caffeine as half a cup of coffee. Realizing that kids sometimes chew several pieces of gum in a row (or at once), the FDA decided to take action. After the meeting, Wrigley's agreed to remove the gum from store shelves. Since then, the FDA has asked food manufacturers to step back while the agency figures out a system for managing caffeine safety in food and beverages. FDA official Michael Taylor asked a question that everyone should consider: "Isn't it time to pause and exercise some restraint?"

Glossary

adenosine a chemical produced naturally in the central nervous system, which builds up each day to cause sleepiness

adverse reaction any harmful side effect of a drug

binge drinking too much over a short period of time

caffeinated containing caffeine, a drug that stimulates the central nervous system

dependence having an emotional or physical need for a drug

depress the effect of drugs that slow down the central nervous system

diabetes a medical condition in which the body cannot control blood sugar levels

dose a measured amount of a drug or medication

drug a substance that changes how the body or brain functions

energy drink a beverage that contains high levels of caffeine and other stimulants, and in some cases alcohol

herbivore an animal that eats plants

interact to mix in unpredictable ways; to have an effect on something else

intoxication a state in which the person feels and acts different after consuming a drug

overdose a large dose of a substance that causes a dangerous reaction in the body

peer pressure words or actions from people of the same age group that suggest a person has to act or look the same to fit in

receptor a specific site on a nerve cell to which neurotransmitters can attach

stimulant a class of drug that speeds up the central nervous system, sometimes taken to increase alertness or energy

synthetic produced in a laboratory

tolerance a reduction in the normal effects of a drug after regular use, requiring a larger dose to obtain the same effect

withdrawal symptoms that occur when a person who is physically dependent stops using a drug

Find Out More

Books

Hasan, Heather. *Caffeine and Nicotine: A Dependent Society.* New York: Rosen Publishing, 2009.

Scott, Elaine. *All About Sleep from A to Zzzz.* New York: Viking, 2008.

Stewart, Melissa. *You've Got Nerve! The Secrets of the Brain and Nerves.* New York: Marshall Cavendish Benchmark, 2011.

Websites

"Can Food Affect Your Child's Behaviour?"

http://www.toronto.ca/health/pdf/nm_child_behaviour.pdf
This website looks at the effects of food additives—caffeine, sugar, food dyes, and more—on children's behavior. Although written for parents, its information is useful to everyone.

How Much Sleep Do I Need?

http://kidshealth.org/teen/your_body/take_care/how_much_sleep.html
TeensHealth covers a variety of health topics relevant

to young people. This page explains the body's need for sleep and how much teens need each night to be healthy.

Neuroscience for Kids - Caffeine

http://faculty.washington.edu/chudler/caff.html

Dr. Eric H. Chudler is a biologist at the University of Washington. His website is designed to help kids better understand the nervous system.

World Anti-Doping Agency Youth Zone (WADA)

http://www.wada-ama.org/en/Education-Awareness/Youth-Zone/

WADA wants you to know the problems with doping in sports and challenges you to make good choices for your own health.

INDEX

Pages in **boldface** are illustrations

About the Author

CHRISTINE PETERSEN has written more than fifty books for young people, covering a wide range of topics in science, health, and social studies. In her free time, Petersen enjoys hiking and snowshoeing with her son near their home in Minneapolis, Minnesota. She is a member of the Society of Children's Book Writers and Illustrators.